Angels, Of Course

A Collection of Illustrated Visits

Win Tuck-Gleason

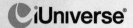

Angels, Of Course

A Collection of Illustrated Visits

Win Tuck-Gleason

To Hannah, Nathan, and Kristina

CONTENTS

LIST OF ILLUSTRATIONS

INTRODUCTION

A lot of thought has gone into deciding how to present the concept of heavenly angels to the general public. When talking to people, I observed that they generally accepted the reality of angels at a distance, but I also discovered most people were not quite comfortable hearing details of their existence in modern times.

I had frequent encounters with angels when I was a child and then again when I was in my twenties and forties. I am finally able to share these episodes and paintings with you. I hope they will make you more aware of the love, guidance, and protection that is available to you.

Angelic presence is very comforting. Angels deliver a very positive atmosphere whenever they are around. A lot of people have felt their presence without being able to see them. So why did I get to see angels? It's a mystery to me. I'm certainly not special. I do, however, come from a long line of Christian ancestry. Maybe my Dutch grandmother prayed them around me.

Being able to see these angels was a wonderful experience; however, actually seeing them was not as important as being dedicated to Jesus Christ.

I want to make it very clear that, as a Christian, one's focus should always be on Christ. Jesus Christ is what Christianity is all about. Angels are His servants only, and we should never worship them. You may never see an angel on earth, and it does not matter one iota.

Sometimes I wonder if Jesus allowed me to see these angels because I needed them so badly to carry me through some of the bad experiences in my life. Don't wish that on yourself!

I don't want to go into detail about some of the things I've been through because they are very personal. Although some reference to them may enable the reader to understand why I might have supernatural protection, I choose to keep most of these experiences private. I would like to keep this account positive and upbeat.

Numerous books about angels are available online and in bookstores. Even *Time* magazine on December 27, 1993, featured angels on their cover with an article. The article stated 60 percent of Americans believe in the existence of angels. People are definitely becoming more interested in angels now than at any other time in history. The number of TV shows and books centered on the subject reflect this fact.

I would like to make it quite clear that I am not a part of the New Age religion. The angels I have seen are the old-fashioned biblical angels. My relationship with angels is more extensive than anyone else's I've heard about, solely in the aspect that I have seen different shapes and sizes of angels.

Angels are emotional. It is very easy to observe their feelings. They communicate their moods. I've heard them play musical instruments, sing, talk, and read. Some angels are invisible but can be felt. I have actually been physically touched by one without being able to see it.

I have seen the results of their invisible actions. On two different occasions, one took over the steering wheel of my car when I was in trouble. At times I knew they were beside me, but I could not see them, and other people could. Very rarely one would speak to me.

The angels I have seen vary in size and configuration. Some wear flowing white gowns and have beautiful wings. This type is similar to the angels generally depicted in artwork. On ceremonial occasions, brilliant crystals or possibly diamonds decorate their gowns. These worship gowns show rank, with epaulets on the shoulders.

I've seen these angels at an average human height or appear to be at least twelve feet tall. There are warrior angels, obviously male, dressed in brown leather, ancient Greek–style uniforms, also with epaulets on the shoulders. They don't have wings. The same height variances occur. Some are regular human height; others appear to be around twelve feet tall.

Then there are what I call my "little companions." They are always in groups of five or eight. They are about three and a half feet tall. They wear little white gowns with hoods covering their heads. They do not have wings either.

There are angels dressed in typical street clothes. They have a presence about them that is not quite human; plus, they appear to have a dual focus. They are aware of the situation around them here as well as somewhere else. They appear and disappear quickly.

There are also very small angels, approximately knee height. They have a translucent, white, cloudlike appearance and resemble chubby little children. They are very happy and loving.

I tried to get an artist to draw some of the forms for me, but I was told I was the only one who could portray them. So I started taking art lessons in September 1994. I could only draw stick people and needed to learn perspective. You will see the paintings that accompany this short manuscript were painted in 1994 and 1995, just as I was getting started.

I noticed all the angels have one thing in common: their faces are quite indistinguishable. For this reason, I have purposefully made the faces vague in the artwork. I actually think an angel helped me with the artwork. I certainly couldn't draw before.

I have spoken at length to different church groups about these experiences and know my talks have made an impact on people's lives. I hope you will keep an open mind while you read this book.

Days of color

Nights of warmth

Golden dawns of promise

Tie me with an invisible thread

To my place in the sun

Win Tuck

February 16, 1983

#1—THE FIRST VISIT

The first recollection of my childhood was angels. I might have been around three years old or possibly a bit younger. I did not, however, carry the memory of them with me through those early years. The thought of them would filter into my mind occasionally, to reappear in full clarity when I was fortysomething. The images started as a blur, almost like the phrase "clearing away the cobwebs," until I could finally remember.

I woke up in a little one-room cabin one warm, breezy summer day. I had been napping in a crib or low bed. The room seemed to have billowing white chiffon curtains swaying through the windows. They were moving in rhythm to a musical sound with a vibration leaving a sensation that I can still feel. The combination of golden light, beautiful music, and warm breeze was very soothing, especially to a young child.

The serenity and quality of sound that registered in my memory at that time I have never heard duplicated, even at a symphonic performance. That sound carried through the little room and filled it to bursting with strings, tinkling cascades, and melodic choruses.

I don't know if that episode occurred once or if it was one of many. All I know is that the beautiful swaying white curtains and the extraordinary music stayed with me all these years. Recollections of them would float into my memory every so often, but I never discussed them with anyone. It was as if I wasn't given permission to talk about them. I never thought about them as being a secret.

This is what happened to bring it into my conscious mind. My mother came down from Canada to visit me where I lived in Delray Beach, Florida, in October 1986. We were enjoying an infrequent visit together, and we started reminiscing about "the good old days" when my dad was still alive and how everything had changed so much since then.

One of the things we talked about was "the seventy acres" on Strawberry Lane, one of the various locations of family farms in the Holland Marsh, Ontario, Canada, an extremely fertile valley consisting of thousands of acres of rich peat moss. My father's family were some of the first pioneers who cleared the land and owned a packing plant that supplied carrots, lettuce, and onions across North America.

On an occasional Saturday, my father would take Mom, my brother, Hal, and me out to check one or another of the family vegetable farms. This particular time I can remember, they put me in the little cabin to rest while they looked over the crops.

I made an idle comment to my mother about the beautiful curtains and the music that was playing and how considerate it was of them to leave me in such nice surroundings.

Mom looked at me in amazement and said, "There were no such things. It was a plain, bare, little work cabin with hardly anything in it."

Well, that wasn't the way I remembered it at all! So I told her all about the gorgeous white swaying curtains, the breezes, the bright sunshine, and the incredible music that played on and on and woke me up from my naps, wonderful memories of comfort and nurture that had come to me from time to time.

We sat quietly disagreeing and agreeing with each other for a while. In the silence of that portion of time, I began to bring into focus the scene I had been unconsciously searching for. I knew with incredible certainly that what I had seen and heard were angels, of course!

Painting B—*Angels Singing to Win (Three Years Old)*

They've been with me off and on all my life, but I never discussed them with anyone. In fact, I don't think I was able. I felt I needed to protect myself and them too. It's difficult to explain. When I think about my angel encounters, I was never permitted to talk about them with anyone until a release time was given.

The release time is an important aspect of my story and explains why I was unable to relate any of these stories before now. I didn't think about the angels after seeing them; neither did I feel compelled to tell anyone. Perhaps I thought, as children can, that everyone saw them.

The angels that visited me when I was around the age of three gave me some incredible gifts. The first is my great love of music. I sang constantly when I was a child. I guess I still do. The second gift was that I never developed a fear of being alone when I was young. Through the years of my childhood, I recall a feeling of being watched over, especially later in my childhood when I was out in the woods or up in the hills. I loved my freedom and spent a lot of time by myself outdoors. I was a wanderer. My father called me "Butterfly." I recall vaguely thinking there were angels around me then. I felt I could talk to whoever wasn't there if I felt like it. They disappeared when I started high school.

The third gift was the certain knowledge that Jesus and heavenly things were real. Therefore, anything anyone told me about God was easy to accept.

My mother agreed with the probability of my first angel story completely. I felt encouraged and able to focus on and remember other visits. It felt strange, as if some unknown source had slowly permitted me to release more experiences.

Sometimes it was years before I could talk about some of them, other times hours. Only once could I say, "They're here right now."

#2—Questioning Faces

By the time I was six years old, we had moved from Aurora, Ontario, to the town of Bradford, where the packing plant was located. I started grade one and piano lessons simultaneously, following a routine where I practiced the piano for a half hour right after school. In our house, the piano was positioned against the wall of a large hall, with a staircase and landing rising directly beside the instrument.

One day during my practicing, I happened to glance sideways, and to my surprise, I saw a dazzling, beautiful, fully recognizable angel of average human height. She was hovering about six inches above the landing at the turn of the stairs. She was watching me with an expectant, questioning expression on her face. I can't remember exactly what she looked like, but she was feminine. She wore a long, full white dress made of thin layers of shiny material with what I thought at the time were sparkles on it. It had a wide, sparkling belt as well.

We stared at each other curiously for a while before she started her upward movement, gliding backward away from me. This angel had beautiful white wings arching over her head behind her back, down her sides, and ending just above the ground. Her wings were motionless when she slowly moved up the stairs and disappeared around a corner.

I thought, *How beautiful*. It left me with a very happy and contented feeling. It was not an invasion of privacy or a frightening experience. The angel was simply there. I continued my practicing and did not even consider telling my mother about the experience, and she was in the kitchen right next to me.

I do not remember seeing another angel for years. I may recall more at a later date.

#3—Angel at the Wheel

The carefree days of my early childhood were gone forever. A neglectful family lifestyle had badly disillusioned and hurt my sunny disposition, which could be an incorrect statement on my part, but one I nevertheless felt. I had gone from being an extroverted child to a tongue-tied young lady. The only way I could express feelings was through the lyrics of the songs I studied.

I married young to get out of the strict household that I felt would not allow me to make my own decisions. And in February 1965, I had been married for two years and had a baby boy named Charles. My husband coached a boys' hockey team, which had qualified to compete in the PeeWee Tournament in Quebec City.

Excitement reigned as kids, parents, and coaches boarded the train. My husband had decided that I would drive our car from Toronto with one of the mothers so we would have a vehicle to use while we were in Quebec City. My religious training had taught me to obey my husband. Those were the days when wives were expected to do what their husbands wanted.

So I picked up the lady around 8:00 a.m. I'd never met her before. We were a little awkward with each other until I found out she was a stay-at-home mom with a slew of kids and entered every contest she could find, winning more trips and toasters than I could imagine ever getting. We had great fun. She entertained me with her stories, and we calculated the twelve-hour drive ahead of us would pass quickly. Wrong!

We never should have left our homes in Toronto. The roads were icy, and driving was treacherous while leaving the city. Optimism ran high. We had packed the car. We were primed and anxious to join our group. We were going!

13

I was driving when we left Toronto. My traveling companion took over at Kingston, Ontario, where we stopped for gas. She had only driven for about an hour when she ran over some black ice on the road and the car went into a 360-degree spinout. This unnerved us both, and after that, she did not drive for the rest of the trip. It was our car, so I decided to drive the rest of the way myself.

It was snowing very hard by the time we crawled into the outskirts of Montreal around 8:00 p.m. We pulled off Highway 401 and revitalized ourselves with French Canadian onion soup at a local restaurant.

We decided we would attempt the trip on to Quebec City, a mere four hours, to join in the fun of the Winter Carnival. Neither of us had ever driven through a snowstorm of this magnitude before, and we were totally unaware of the involved dangers.

We couldn't find an open gas station for refueling when we turned off the highway, so we started on the road toward Drummondville, thinking we could get gas there. The drive seemed to go on forever. I still have the Drummondville road signs embedded in my brain.

We finally reached the town around 10:45 p.m., only to find it completely shut down. No restaurants, gas stations, or motels were open. We thought there was no alternative but to continue. We left the lights of the town behind us to resume crawling behind the other vehicles plodding along the single, snow-covered track of a four-lane highway.

My traveling companion eventually fell asleep, leaving me bleary-eyed, exhausted, and frightened. I worried about our gas supply. Cars were pulling off the road ahead of us, forcing me to go around them.

I started praying over and over, "Please help us. Don't let me fall asleep. Don't let me follow any other cars off the road."

I was staring at the snowflakes hitting the windshield, praying, glancing at the fuel gauge, watching the snowdrifts getting bigger, and praying some more. There was nothing but static on the radio. My space was definitely getting smaller and more isolated.

Suddenly I had an incredible sensation! At first, I couldn't recognize what it was. After a minute or two, I realized I was sitting on a lap, a very comfortable and solid one. I was lifted about four inches off the seat because I could see the road ahead of me from a higher angle. I could feel control of the steering wheel shift into stronger hands than mine. This was amazing, and I wasn't the least bit frightened, although I did keep a hand on the steering wheel. I enjoy having a vivid imagination, but this experience went beyond imagination.

I relaxed and began to enjoy this incredibly comfortable lap. I knew it was an angel that had come to help us. I wanted to wake up my friend, but she was sleeping peacefully. I figured she would think I was hallucinating, so I enjoyed it all by myself. I could shift around on this generous lap and turn and look into the back seat. I was at peace and enjoying myself.

We reached the suburbs of Quebec City after 2:00 a.m. My friend woke up when I stopped for directions at a twenty-four-hour welcome center. She looked around in amazement, quite stunned, I think, at the height of the snow. I still didn't say anything to her about the help we had to get through it. The angel had disappeared when we got back into the car. I had to drive again.

The directions, which the staff working the desk at the welcome center had given us, took us down the highway and across a wide river over an old steel bridge. The wind was blowing huge snowdrifts across the opening, making the tall girders look like the entrance of a dark tunnel. After careful consideration, we chickened out.

Just up ahead and to our left, we could make out lights in what we rightly assumed was a bridge gatehouse. It was open, so we pulled in for advice.

The attendant said, "Don't cross over on your own. Wait till morning."

We didn't like the sound of that after traveling so far.

He added, "If you insist on crossing, wait until you see a huge truck coming. Get right up close behind it, and follow it across. But there aren't any trucks running this time of night. It could be a long wait."

Undaunted, we got the car into position. About one minute later and before we had time to lose our nerve, an eighteen-wheeler came thundering along the road toward the bridge. We fearlessly fell in behind it and crossed over the river in a huge billow of snow to the safety of benign and sleeping Quebec City. Finding the hotel was easy, and we finally filled the gas tank the next morning.

On reflection, I have a feeling that angels were driving the truck that appeared just when we needed it.

#4—THE NEWS

On March 4, 1965, three weeks later, I was standing in the kitchen doing the dinner dishes. My husband had gone out to a hockey game, and the baby was in bed. It was around 7:00 p.m. While I was staring out into the cold night with the snow swirling around, a voice spoke to me. The sound was directly in front of my face, as if it was coming from the window over the sink. It was a baritone voice, well timbered and mature, very authoritative and kind.

The voice said, "Your father just died." The message was unmistakable.

I slipped off my rubber gloves, walked into the darkened living room, sat down on the couch, and waited for the phone to ring. It did.

My brother, Hal, was on the line. Our parents, along with my little sister, Hendi, were staying with him and his wife, Jan, in Ottawa, Ontario. Whenever Hal phoned, he always had a boisterous, happy attitude, but not this time.

"Can I speak to Chuck?" he very quietly asked.

I knew Hal wanted to give Chuck the news to relay to me, to soften the blow of him telling me the devastating news of my dad dying so suddenly.

I didn't want to startle Hal by saying that I already knew why he was calling, so I replied in the same tone, "He's at a game."

"What's your mother-in-law's phone number?"

I gave it to him without question, and he hung up. So I continued my vigil on the couch and waited. About a half hour later, the doorbell rang. My mother-in-law and best girlfriend, Fran, were at the door. They just walked in, came into the living room, sat down on either side of me, held my hands, and confirmed the message.

"Your dad died of heart failure at seven this evening."

I didn't tell them I already knew either.

#5—Good News Too

Years later, with a lot of changes in our lives, I was a vulnerable single parent, having gone through a nerve-racking divorce four years earlier. Our only child, Charles, was in grade nine. I moved into a beautiful duplex in North Toronto, near the Lawrence and Yonge subway station. We chose this area specifically so Charles could go to Lawrence Park Collegiate and use the subway system.

One evening he did not come home on time from an appointment. He was a couple of hours late. I was completely frantic. I'd never been so frightened in my entire life. So I alerted my mom. She and my stepdad drove right over.

Before they arrived, I went next door and told my neighbor Bernie. He came back home with me and did the best thing: he reminded me of the faith I talked about sometimes.

He said, "Pray. Have you prayed yet?" As a vice president of a shipping line, he was used to handling security issues, and this was what he said.

He stayed with me for a little while and then left. I was embarrassed that it took someone I didn't think paid much attention to God to remind me to pray.

My heart was pounding. I finally lay flat out on the floor and prayed, "Please help."

The same rich voice from years before immediately spoke again. "Charles is safe."

My fears disappeared immediately! And Charles came home just after 9:00 p.m.

He had gone straight from his appointment to his part-time job at a local bookstore. I didn't know he was scheduled to work that night.

#6—THE LADDER

About a year later, Hendi, my younger sister, was staying with us. One afternoon I was playing some sacred music on the piano in the living room when she happened to walk into the room. There, she recounted later, she saw angels climbing up and down a ladder over my head while I was playing. I was totally unaware of them. I couldn't understand what she meant.

She quoted from the story of Jacob's ladder in the Bible (Genesis 28:12), "And he dreamed, and behold a ladder set up on the earth, and the top of it reached to heaven: and behold the angels of God ascending and descending on it."

#7—"Get a Job"

Charles and I had a wonderful life. We traveled a lot. I had a beautiful hunter that I boarded at Leitchcroft, a local riding stable. I'd always wanted my own horse. So I took English riding lessons and rode well enough to hunt.

While he was growing up, Charles and I skied in the winter and sailed or went to the cottage in the summer when we could get away. Plus, he went to camp during the summer holidays.

I worked at various jobs but didn't have a "career." My interest was music. I always wanted to be a classical singer. Before I was married, I worked toward my artist diploma and practiced at the Royal Conservatory every school day with Dr. Ernesto Vinci, a highly respected voice teacher at the University of Toronto. He wanted me to continue my studies in Milan, Italy. It was all I could dream about, but my father wouldn't allow it. He said I could sing for the Lord, but not on the stage!

He was a very powerful man, and I would never go against his wishes. No matter who tried to change his mind, forget it. It was a waste of time. I lost heart, pretty much gave up on music, and got married.

Years earlier, even when I was in my late teens, when I did things that displeased my father, he would make an appointment with me at the dining room table for me to meet him in his library at a specific time, usually two or three days away.

So in addition to being chewed out for some misdemeanor, I would also have to suffer through the waiting period. This could possibly work with an employee, but with a daughter, it just resulted in tears.

Years later, as a result of making hasty decisions and having to settle for changed career plans, I had a problem: I did not have a goal, and I was using up my inheritance.

I was moaning and groaning to God in prayer one day about how I needed more money, and I must admit I fully expected a miracle of some kind.

Then the voice came back. It said, "Get a job!"

"What?" I yelped. This couldn't be true!

"You heard me. Get a job!"

It was such a beautiful, richly timbered voice, and it was said in such kindly humor that I couldn't be offended. He was absolutely right.

Well, one can't argue with that. So I got a job.

#8—ANGELS AND DEMONS

I would be very remiss if I didn't tell you the downside of encountering angels. Like light and dark, good and evil, all things have their opposite. The same rule applies to angels.

To be very basic, there are two groups of angels. There are angels of the Lord: heavenly messengers, ministering angels, and guardian angels. There are different types, some with ranks and names. These angels are related to heaven and God. We read about them in the Bible. Then there are the fallen angels, called devils, demons, and evil spirits. These are related to hell and the devil.

Before the world was created, Satan was one of God's favorite angels. But he attempted a coup to overthrow God. (References to the fall of Satan, the prince of this world, were researched from the Holy Bible.)

As a result of the mighty battle in heaven, Satan and a third of all the angels were thrown out. The rest stayed in heaven to serve God. It is very important to be aware of the numbers. Two-thirds of the angels stayed to serve God, and one-third became Satan's servants.

Both angels and demons are present on earth. Angels take directions from God and carry out His instructions to help His children on earth. Likewise, demons carry out Satan's commands to destroy.

It is not my intention to outline Satan's entire history. This is a simple attempt to make you aware that there are devils out there as well as angels. And I have seen some of them as well. Understand there are both good and evil influences here on earth. We need to recognize them. Prayer is your biggest weapon. The most important fact to remember is that God is good. He won!

Romans 8:38–39 reads, "And I am convinced that nothing can ever separate us from God's love. Neither death nor life, neither angels nor demons, neither our fears for today nor our worries about tomorrow—not even the powers of hell can separate us from God's love."

When you are afraid, call Jesus Christ's name out loud. The Bible says, "Every knee shall bow at the name of Jesus. In heaven and on earth and under the earth" (Philippians 2:10).

#9—LITTLE COMPANIONS

In 1983, I separated from my second husband and moved back to Toronto, Canada. After sorting through a lot of problems, we decided to try again. This is where the fun begins.

In November 1983, I had a large U-Haul trailer packed and my car loaded, and I was ready to go back to Houston. I had been staying at my sister's place, on the twentieth floor of an apartment building in Mississauga, a suburb of Toronto.

Our mother came for a visit the night before. She was very concerned about me attempting such a long trip by myself, especially towing a heavy trailer in the snow. Now my mother can really pray. She gets amazing results.

She had been repeatedly looking out of the window down at the heavily packed car and trailer parked at the curb below because she was concerned someone would break into them.

Suddenly she said, "It's okay now. Little angels are standing around your car and trailer."

Right! I thought. We didn't check.

The following morning, she did it again. She said, "The little angels are still there, around the car and trailer, just walking back and forth."

We sort of laughed at her. We didn't check again and then got caught up in the confusion of saying goodbye.

Now it was time to leave. My destination that night was to get as far as Indianapolis, six hundred miles ahead. Plus, I still had to go through American Customs and Immigration in Detroit.

Later that night, about 150 miles before Indy, I was driving along in the dark, listening to the radio. Suddenly up ahead, just at the outer limit of the headlight beam, I saw this little white thing floating above the ground, keeping at the front of the beam of light. I couldn't figure out what it was. I wasn't tired. I had just finished having a light dinner break and a cup of coffee. So what was this? It was a solid-white elongated mass about three feet long and a foot and a half around with what looked like an arm. Pointing forward!

Painting C—*Traveling to Indy*

I was making good time and kept up the same pace. Suddenly the funniest thing happened! A little angel was sitting directly in front of me, straddling the casing of the headlight on the hood. It looked like it was riding a horse. It was having a wonderful time waving its arm over its head. It had the same conformation as the first one.

I looked out of the passenger-side window and saw one floating beside the car. I looked in the rearview mirror and could observe two little angels sitting on the roof of the U-Haul. One was reading a newspaper, and the other one looked as if it were playing cards or some sort of game. None of the five had wings. They all looked exactly alike. All wore full-length gowns with hoods.

I could not believe what I was seeing. As you can imagine, by this time I was very alert. It was such a hilarious scene that it made me laugh out loud. I kept looking back and forth from the one up front on point to the side guard and back to the top of the U-Haul. It was a wonderful feeling. These were the little angels Mom had seen before I left Toronto. I realized they were along to protect and guide me. We drove like that all the way to the outskirts of Indianapolis.

That was my introduction to my little companions. They stayed with me on and off for three years. These little guys were a source of joy for me while I lived in Texas. They would appear every so often, quite unexpectedly, for a little visit.

One time I was busy vacuuming the kitchen one Saturday morning. I turned my gaze toward the dining room, and there they were, eight of them, lolling around in all sorts of positions on a bleacher. Some were lying sideways, one was resting its chin on its hands, and a few were watching me. Another was looking out of the window. The general expressions on their faces were "Boring!"

Sometimes they would drive along in the car when I went to the office. One particular day in Houston, I was having a meeting with a photographer. We were having an animated disagreement over how to display a piece of equipment. Neither of us would compromise. I happened to glance over to the window, and there they were! The little angels were on their bleacher, all eight of them, jumping up and down, waving their little arms in encouragement, cheering me on.

They were just under four feet tall, dressed in the little white gowns with hoods, the same as the other ones. They did not have wings either. They did, however, have a portable bleacher! They somehow took it with them. They used it in a lot of places, including the dining room and my office, but not in the car. In the car, they all crowded into the back seat and grinned at me. We did have some brief eye contact but nothing intense. I definitely knew they were looking at me, and I was aware of everything that was going on.

This was another hilarious sight, which I still laugh about all these years later. Anyway, to get back to the story, their presence made me feel confident that I was handling the photo session in the appropriate way. I got what I wanted.

On many occasions, I would be working quietly at my desk, and they would be lounging around on their bleacher, snoozing, or reading small newspapers. They were great company for me. I really looked forward to their visits. They would appear and disappear. They would always be in groups of five or eight, never alone. They stayed out of the bathroom and bedroom. They never invaded my privacy. They never spoke to me either.

Circumstances had moved my husband and me to Boca Raton, Florida, and the little angels came along. After being there for a few months, I heard about a local church that sounded interesting.

One Sunday morning, I decided to attend a service, and my little companions came with me. We were all standing crowded together at the back of the church. I was not in a hurry because I was looking for a place to sit. Suddenly they all left me. They dashed off and joined two huge bleachers of little angels that looked exactly like they did, up in the front left side of the sanctuary. It was an amazing sight. They were all singing and waving their arms along with the church music.

This is where they abandoned me. They stayed at the church. I guess they figured their job was finished since they had led me to a terrific church. I attended that church for two years, from 1985 to 1987, until I returned to Canada after my second marriage ended.

During that time, they would come and visit me when I was in church. They would find me wherever I was sitting. Usually five at a time would crowd in around me, stay for a five-minute visit to encourage me, and then leave again. I really enjoyed them. I think the people sitting right next to me were totally unaware of the little heavenly visitors pressing against my legs and sitting on my lap.

I took my turn as part of a singing group up on the front platform and could see the congregation very well from up there. Once I saw the little angels around another person, a woman who had just been diagnosed with a breast tumor, and special prayers were being said for her. They were crushing in close around her with worried looks on their faces.

Painting E—*Reading on Their Bleacher*

I often thought about what a strange shape they were. The fact that they looked like Casper, the comic ghost, made me think someone else had seen them also.

One day I went into a print shop in Boca Raton to get some work done. While I was waiting for some information, I happened to browse through a basket of small notepads left out for customers. One of the notepads was printed with a drawing of the little angels. You can imagine my surprise and delight. I took one of the pages but didn't ask where it had come from. I wish I had. It would have been wonderful to talk to someone besides my mother about these little guys.

Painting F—*Outline Sketch on Notepad at Print Shop in Boca Raton* (Background by Win Tuck)

#10—Raising the Roof

The second Sunday, I went to the same church. I noticed the appearance of the sanctuary was different from on the previous Sunday. This is difficult to explain.

My first impression of the sanctuary interior was how high the ceiling appeared to be and how bright the room was. When I saw it for the second time, the dimensions had changed. The ceiling was lower. It had dropped to regular height for the proportions of the room.

I stared at the windows and ceiling for a while, trying to figure out what the difference was.

Then it occurred to me: the previous Sunday, I had seen white-robed angels about six feet tall standing on the four walls of the sanctuary, holding the roof up over their heads.

So the roof was actually raised approximately eight feet higher, letting in extra light as well. The angels had literally "raised the roof." This only happened the first time I attended the church.

Painting G—*Raising the Roof*

#11—WARRIOR ANGELS

I began attending this same church regularly and joined the choir. A group of about ten singers at a time would take turns singing up on the platform for the morning service. I loved taking my turn, but for the most part, I sat with the congregation.

The church had large, clear glass windows on both sides of the sanctuary. Quite often these windows would be open, letting in the balmy breezes. On one side was a beautiful little lake with a surrounding patio, flower garden, and palm trees. The other side had gardens and a parking lot. One could sit in the sanctuary and see out both sides of the building.

I happened to glance out of the windows facing the parking lot, where I saw a company of angel troops along the entire side of the church. They were all dressed in brown leather. As closely as I can describe them, they looked like ancient Greek warriors.

They were wearing leather tunics with two-and-a-half-inch vertical leather panels forming a kilt of some sort, which ended just above the knee. They wore leather sandals on their feet with leather laces crossing up to their knees. Heavy leather belts held sheathed swords or daggers. They had leather sashes crossing their chests from their shoulders to their waistbands. They all wore leather helmets and carried shields. Plus, their uniforms had epaulets indicating rank on their shoulders. They stood in small groups, with a leader in front of each group. They appeared to be very tense and seemed to be waiting for something to happen.

I turned to look out of the other side windows and saw more angels along that side as well. They were very alert; both groups were watching the church. They stayed at their posts during the service and left before the people came out.

Painting H—*Warrior Angels on Alert* (painted in the style of Cézanne)

Another time I was on the platform, singing with the group. I saw the same angels out on the patio by the lake. They were standing around in small groups, casually watching. I did not sense any tension this time.

People were walking back and forth across the patio, making preparations for a coffee hour that followed the service. I was amazed to observe that the people did not bump into the angels. I watched them for quite a while. People diverted their way around the angels. It was quite comical to observe. The people must have sensed their presence, but no one I spoke to later mentioned seeing them.

I would just like to mention again the difference in attitude between the first and second time I saw them around the church. On the first visit, I observed that they appeared to be on the offensive, tense and watching for some sort of attack. They were definitely on guard. Against what? I don't know.

The second time, they appeared to be relaxed, enjoying the gardens and sunshine, acting more like guardians.

#12—The Intruder

I was on my own again, this time for good. I moved from a condo on the Intercoastal in Boca Raton to a quiet street in Delray Beach that was lined with some old Banyan trees. The attraction for me was the eighty-foot-span Banyan tree in the front garden and an orange tree in the back garden. It had a small Florida room at the front of the cottage, where I watched television.

One Sunday night around 11:00 p.m., I got up from watching a movie and looked out of the front window for what I thought was no apparent reason. I watched a tall man with long blond hair and no shirt on walk across my front lawn and go around the corner of the house. I went into the bedroom on that side and watched him walk past the window and around the corner to the back. I went into the dining room and observed him go over to the door and put his hand on the doorknob.

I was standing at the open, screened-in dining room window with the light of the Florida room behind me. I started talking out loud. "He's trying to get in!"

I wasn't the least bit afraid. Under normal circumstances, I would have been terrified, but the invisible angel that had summoned me to the window to watch this person's progress around the house had stayed at my side as I went from room to room. So it was quite natural for me to talk to it.

It didn't say anything out loud to me, and I couldn't see it, but the intruder did. He was rooted to the spot with his hand on the doorknob, and he stared at us for what seemed like ages. The look on his face was total disbelief. He finally bolted off into the darkness of the trees in the backyard.

I ran to a window at the side of the house where I could shout for my neighbor. I yelled out what had happened and gave a description of the man. My neighbor ran back into the house to get some sort of weapon and his dog. Then he tore off after the intruder. I was very surprised at his reaction.

My neighbor didn't catch him, thank goodness. When he came back, he told me a person with the same description—tall with long blond hair and no shirt—had been burglarizing houses in the neighborhood for almost two years and no one had ever caught him.

I went to bed with the window open and slept like a baby.

#13—Flight Guardian

I was still living in the cute little Hemmingway-style cottage under the Banyan tree in Delray Beach. My mother came down for a three-week visit from Canada. She is such a Christian lady, and the focus of her conversation is frequently about sacred things. We had a wonderful time exchanging experiences and things we had learned. I told her many of my angel stories, and she delighted in them.

Two very interesting things happened during her visit: the first was negative and the second was incredible.

I worked as a store manager at the local mall. One day as I was leaving the back entrance of the building and heading toward my car, I saw a strange little creature. It darted from under the side of the hood, directly across my path, and disappeared into nothing.

It was about three feet high, hunched over to look smaller than it was. It was black and gray with very skinny arms and legs. The body appeared to be round because of its clothes, which were dirty, tattered remnants, flapping around and behind it as it ran. I instinctively felt it was a little devil and worried that it might have done something to my car. I carefully inspected the outside and sort of looked under it. I said a prayer for safety and drove home.

That evening after dinner, I got up to clear away the dishes. The same little black figure darted out from under the table as I moved my chair back. It ran past me, tatters flapping behind it, and disappeared through the wall. It was very disconcerting. I told Mom what had just happened and about the same little figure appearing earlier in the day. We prayed about it, and it never came back.

The second episode occurred when I took Mom to the airport in Ft. Lauderdale, after she had already boarded the carrier to return home. The plane had taxied away from the terminal and was standing about three hundred feet from the viewing window, where I was watching. Suddenly I could see a huge figure. It was at least twelve feet tall. It was a warrior angel, but over twice as tall as the ones I saw at the church. Other than his great height, he looked the same. He was dressed in the same brown leather uniform of the ancient soldiers. However, he must have been a high-ranking officer. He had a lot of seniority on his epaulets. He was huge.

He was casually standing in the busy ground space, intently watching men load the plane. He moved around, turning to see everything that was going on. No one bumped into him; vehicles maneuvered around him.

I was so surprised that I shouted out loud, but no one paid any attention to me. It was fascinating. I waited and watched as the plane taxied away around the corner. Then I followed its path to the end of the building. It was a fairly long walk to the end corner of the terminal, and it took me a few minutes to get there.

When I finally did, the plane was way out on the runway with other planes. One of the planes had the huge angel standing on top of it, just in front of the upright tailpiece. I figured that was the plane Mom was on. The angel kept standing there while the plane took off and disappeared from sight.

That night, when I knew she must have arrived home, I phoned her and told her about the angel.

She said, "I know. I could feel its presence." Then she added, "When the flight attendant gave the announcements over the microphone, he ended with saying, 'We'll have a good flight. God is with us.'"

Neither of us have ever heard a flight attendant say anything like that before or since.

Mom said she had a wonderful flight home.

I guess so!

Painting I—*Flight Guardian*

#14—Christmas Worship Angels

This story is difficult to tell, as I need to describe not only the visual experience but also the feelings it evoked.

This was the first Christmas I had ever been on my own. My second marriage had finally ended in June. My entire family was up north, including my son, Charles, whom I especially wanted to be with for the holidays. Not only that, my telephone was not working properly. I was not getting any calls. I'll explain later.

I was working extra long hours, and to partially compensate for my loneliness, I had invited some people from work over for Christmas dinner. I had a beautiful Christmas tree decorated with shells and bows and prepared all the traditional food, including a big turkey, for dinner.

I did not receive any Christmas cards or phone calls from my family. However, I received eleven Christmas presents from unexpected sources, including neighbors and friends. Receiving gifts from anyone other than my immediate family was very unusual. It's never happened before or since. These acts of kindness floored me and made me feel wonderful, but I could not understand why I had not heard from my family. And with all these things on my mind, even though I was mentally and physically exhausted, I wanted to go to church.

Christmas Eve is a very sensitive time. Families prepare for the celebration the following day, and lonely people reflect on their loss at this time. By 11:00 p.m. this night, most people are exhausted. Some folks are at home, others are trying to get there, and some are in various church services around the country. Almost everyone feels anticipation. The excitement of what tomorrow will bring is on most people's minds. At church, even though it's late, the feeling is very reverent on this especially holy night.

After work, I met a friend for a late dinner, and then we both went to the service. Banks of red poinsettia and white Christmas lights decorated the front of the church. The communion table was simple by contrast. Beautiful Christmas carols filled our hearts and called us to worship. The familiar songs and words recalled many feelings of thankfulness throughout the years.

A gentleness descended on the congregation. Then, as people were slowly going forward to take communion, I saw two angels appear on either side of the platform. Then I observed four shining angels suspended without movement at the front of the sanctuary. They had miraculously shimmered into focus. The feeling they emitted was one of intense reverence and worship. They were in awe. Their focus was not in this room. They were awestruck with something other than the scene before them.

Apparently, these angels were expressing very intense feelings of love and devotion to the remembrance of the birth of Christ. They were recognizing His supremacy and godhead by their total concentration and worshipful attitude; plus, they were honoring Him by dressing themselves in their finest robes, the beautiful worship gowns.

The angels were approximately twice as tall as the ministers serving communion. I figure they were twelve feet tall. I could see their gowns and hair in detail, but once again their faces were hard to distinguish, although they appeared to be masculine.

They were dressed in splendid ceremony gowns of iridescent white, encrusted with sparkling, colored jewels with a lot of either diamonds or crystals. Their gowns hung down approximately a yard below their feet. I could make out the dents where their toes were. The gowns had jeweled epaulets on the shoulders and the familiar crisscross bands across their chests, this time in sparkling jewels. Their wings arched behind their backs and hung down their sides, ending just above their feet.

They were motionless. They were simply and magnificently there. These four angels were the most beautiful sight I have ever seen. Even though they did not move, the energy they created radiated throughout the sanctuary, causing the congregation to quiet down and become very worshipful. People were drawn close to each other. They were more kindly, generous, and reverent. It was indeed a very holy night.

I was sitting about halfway down the sanctuary and had time to observe them. I was unable to tell my friend they were there. I could only marvel at them by myself. These beautiful angels appeared in the church to celebrate the birth of the Christ child. As far as I know, other than myself, no one saw them. But their presence did not go unnoticed.

I have to say it again: the feeling of awe and worship they showed to me emanated and encompassed the congregation as well. The service became inspired, strengthening and renewing the people. Their attitudes and countenances began to reflect those of the angels. A sense of reverence, worship, and certainty descended on the congregation.

Painting J—*Christmas Eve Worship Angels*

This feeling sustained me on my drive home and all the next day. On December 26, I discovered the telephone ringer had been turned off. I'd never done that before. When the postman came, he delivered a pile of cards, letters, and packages from home. Had this happened through human error? Had angels saved my Christmas?

Footnote

I had a vision that explains the importance of the worship gowns the angels wore. It is a clear scene of a great many angels working in a long, low, open-sided building. They are very busily working at individual tables with some sort of sewing machine apparatus. They are actually making the worship gowns in a frenzy of activity to meet a deadline. Materials are piled up on nearby tables. Thousands of finished gowns are hanging in long rows.

The gowns are being prepared for the great wedding feast. These are the gowns the angels will wear at the end celebration of time when Jesus, the Bridegroom, brings His church to heaven. The church is the bride of Christ.

#15—Mood Lifters

A couple of months later in the spring of 1987, I was singing with the group again up on the platform before the service started. We had two soloists who occasionally sang together. This was fairly unusual, as they could be quite competitive. This particular morning, they were singing together but were at opposite sides of the platform with about twenty feet between them.

Their expressions were serious even though the song was quite upbeat. Suddenly I saw a mist around their feet. This turned into a dense, low cloud, which formed into at least fifty tiny angels dressed in little white gowns. They looked like chubby little children about a year or two old.

They slowly pushed the two singers toward each other. As they moved together, the soloists began to smile and nod to each other and to the congregation. By the time the song was finished, they were laughing and turning to laugh with the musicians and then the congregation. Throughout this, the little angels were also milling around and smiling. They put everyone in a good mood.

The music director, one of the singers, turned to me and mouthed, "Are they here?"

I nodded yes. Later he said he could feel them but couldn't see them.

#16—THE DRUMMERS

Another Sunday when I was in the chorus, we were singing a particularly rhythmic song that had a difficult bongo solo in it. While the drummer was playing, I glanced over at him and saw two motionless "men" on either side of him. Looking straight ahead, they were dressed in regular clothes and were the same height as the drummer. When he was finished playing, they disappeared.

Later I spoke to him and asked if he had been aware of anything next to him. He said he knew they were there but could not see them.

#17—The Request

On subsequent Christmas Eves, I have looked for other angels in other churches, never seeing anything to match the splendor of 1986.

I moved back to the Toronto area to be with my son, Charles, in April 1987. Since leaving Florida, I have seen angels on different occasions in Toronto, Tottenham, and Collingwood, Ontario.

That spring, Charles's father and I met in his office to discuss Charles's graduation from college. I could feel the presence of an angel near me and actually turned around in my seat to look behind a large floor plant that was there. A four-foot-tall mature-looking angel in white was poking through the leaves, staring at me.

I wondered, *What's up?*

Sure enough, Chuck Sr. made a derogatory remark that hurt me, and I was ready to retort back in kind. But the angel stopped me. It became very agitated and waved its arms in sweeping motions, which indicated to me not to say anything. This caught my attention, diverting it from what big Chuck was saying, and I decided not to answer him.

What was the use of ruining a graduation celebration? Nothing. Charles needed both of his parents there.

That summer I was the substitute pianist for three weeks at the church I was attending. Try as I might, I could not get the congregation to sing enthusiastically. I turned my head slightly during one of the songs and saw a semitranslucent female angel with a woebegone expression on her face standing beside the piano, looking sadly at the congregation. I knew nothing great was going to be happening here. I left that church shortly after that.

That Christmas Eve, in a different church in Tottenham, I could hardly wait to go to church! During the service, I looked everywhere for some angels but could not see any. I was getting upset at the thought of there not being any at the service. I began to pray, "Please, God, let me see some angels." Nothing. "Please let there be some angels here," I prayed again.

Then I felt their presence. I turned around in the pew and looked way up into the rafters at the back of the sanctuary. About ten of them of were there. They appeared almost transparent, looking reluctant to be there and not a part of the service. They conveyed they were only there in answer to my need to see them and would rather be somewhere else. They had faded away by the next time I looked.

Those were two different times in Tottenham where the angels seemed to be fading away from me. I wondered what that meant.

The next Christmas Eve, in the same church, I knew better than to ask to see them, but I couldn't help myself. I prayed to see them again, and a little worship angel came and stood at my side for about ten minutes and then left. Every year I pray to God that I'll see the worship angels in their lavish gowns again, but I haven't yet.

We visited the same church in Florida for the Christmas Eve service in 1993, but I did not see any angels at the church. I did, however, see warrior angels lining Atlantic Boulevard in Delray Beach when we were on our way to the hotel.

#18—Take the Wheel

That first winter back in Canada, around 10:30 one night, I was heading for my home near Tottenham during a hazardous snowstorm, the first I'd experienced in many years. Driving along Highway 9, approximately two or three miles from Strawberry Lane, just west of Highway 400 in the Holland Marsh, the road was reduced to a blanket of snow.

No tracks were ahead of me in the snow. I came down a slight pitch, and in the distance ahead of me, I could see approaching lights. They looked like they were in my lane. Obviously, the driver of the approaching car could not figure out where the road was either. I started panicking. The vehicle kept getting closer. I slowed down but didn't get off the road.

Suddenly the steering wheel turned clockwise sharply, jerking my body to the right. The oncoming car flew by. My steering wheel quickly turned back to the left, bringing me right back into my lane.

It was over in a couple of seconds. I know I did not do this!

The next day, I went back and stopped to check the spot where the mishap had occurred, and I discovered a deep ditch right beside the road. If the car had not turned back onto the road immediately, I would have ended up in the ditch. I was unaware of this situation the previous night. Therefore, I concluded that an unseen angel had helped me out again.

#19—GUARDIAN ANGELS

Company of 100

Jim, my third husband, entered my life in 1990, and we moved to Collingwood, Ontario, in May 1992, where we live in a condo house in a resort area. Even though the neighbors were there most of the time, it occasionally seemed quite desolate. Jim travels for business quite a lot.

One summer night around 11:00, I was alone and fretting a bit, looking out of an open upstairs window, when to my delight I could suddenly see shiny, brightly clad, human-height angels, packed shoulder to shoulder, crowding the entire back lawn. They were giving off a glow that filled the yard and brightened the space about fifteen feet high. I ran to the front and looked out over our little court. They were on the lawn and filled that space there as well.

I haven't had to worry about being alone here either.

Two Snowplows

In January 1994, I drove along with Jim in the morning to do some shopping in Toronto. The weather was all right when we left Collingwood, but it got progressively worse as we headed south. Jim went to his office in Georgetown, and I continued on my way. We planned to drive back to Collingwood in the evening.

At noon I phoned him, and we decided to stay at the Delta Inn, a large hotel just off the 401 Highway in Mississauga, for the night. The traffic was crawling along, and the municipal snowplows could not keep the roads clear. Traffic had almost stopped.

I drove south toward the 401, got mixed up, and had to take the North Service Road to get on the big highway. The service road was in far worse condition than the main streets were. As I was making my entrance onto this road, suddenly a large, smart-looking taupe-colored Jeep with a snowplow on it caught my eye as it zipped across my path from the other direction and sped off in front of me. I laughed out loud.

I knew immediately this was no ordinary Jeep. Angels were driving it. First, we don't have snowplows like that around here. Instead we have the great big yellow-and-black ones. Second, I've never seen a private jeep equipped with a plow like that on public roads in the city, especially with its side windows open. I could see the driver and a passenger were laughing and swaying as they sped by.

I wanted to get a closer look and sped up, but it pulled ahead faster than I dared drive. It was quite a long way to the next interchange. By the time I reached it, the Jeep had disappeared, but I was driving on their plowed path.

Thanks, guys!

#20—ANGELS IN AGREEMENT

The last angels I have seen were in the church I attend in Collingwood, Ontario. It was during a Lenten service. They appeared very suddenly at a specific time during the sermon when the minister spoke of compassion, referring to Pontius Pilate. The concept of feeling sorry for Pontius Pilate startled me, but I was struck with a strong feeling of certainty that this was correct because that is exactly what their countenance portrayed, compassion. It seemed to me that the angels agreed with what the minister was saying. Their facial expressions mirrored affirmation.

I was in the choir loft behind the minister. Angels were hanging over our heads, high up in the rafters, with ten on either side of the sanctuary. Twenty suspended angels, all dressed in plain white robes, hung in midair with their backs at the same angle as the slanted roof. They appeared to be leaning against the ceiling. They did not have wings.

Because their bodies were at an angle, their extra-long sleeves hung straight down toward the floor. It was an amazing sight. They did not move a muscle and stayed like that during the sermon.

CONCLUSION

I never know when angels are going to appear. I have learned to look at the circumstances surrounding the occasions very carefully. I have observed that the angels always give me confidence and a feeling of security and happiness. It's still a mystery as to why I see all these angels; I can't explain it all. Maybe after this book starts touching lives, we will have more answers.

I believe the spirit of Jesus Christ guided me to write this book. For some reason, He touched my life in a profound way by letting me see angels. I believe He wanted me to record my angel stories so some good news could be heard about Him and people could be aware of angels in their lives and feel the closeness of the kingdom of heaven in our world, even if they can't see them.

The reality of heaven can fortify the brokenhearted,

proclaim freedom for the restrained,

and comfort those who grieve.

The closeness of heaven to earth can provide for those who grieve in the world

to endow on them a crown of beauty instead of guilt.

The healing powers of gladness instead of defeat.

A reason to praise instead of having a spirit of despair.

Arguments against organized religion have merit. People blame God for things that go wrong. That's a lie that the devil started. God gives people the freedom of choice. Satan enslaves.

Through the centuries, many people have been close to God, and they can be compared to great oaks in a garden, a planting of the Lord for the display of His splendor. In His faithfulness, He rewards them and makes a promise, and their offspring will be acknowledged as people the Lord has blessed.

Even as the earth produces a garden, likewise God makes righteousness and praise spring up before all the people of the world.

BIBLIOGRAPHY

Connolly, David. *In Search of Angels*. New York: Putnam, 1993.

Graham, Billy. *Angels God's Secret Agents*. Dallas: Word, 1975.

Holy Bible, King James Version.

NLT Life Application Study Bible. Tyndale.

These original sacred paintings are not for sale. The collection is on permanent display in a church in Melbourne, Florida. Special arrangements can be made with churches to host a temporary exhibit for fundraising.

Contact Win@FineArtbyWinTuck.com.

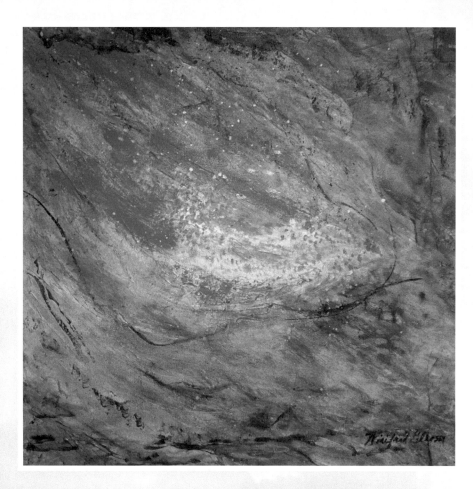

Angel #1 By Win Tuck-Gleason

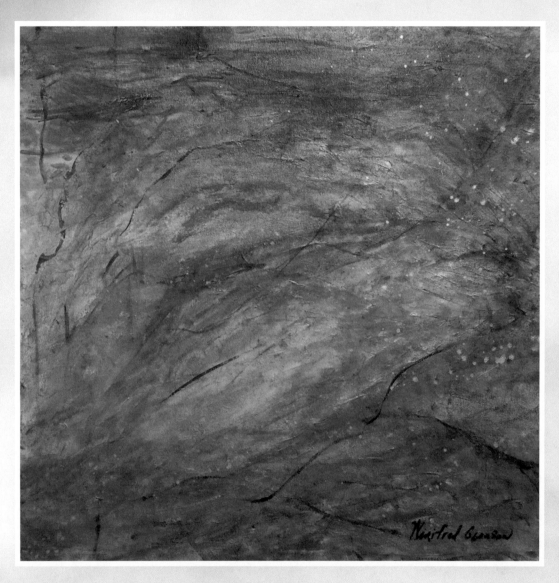

Angel #2 By Win Tuck-Gleason

Birth of Jesus — Luke 2 By Win Tuck-Gleason

Christmas Angel - reverse painting By Win Tuck-Gleason

Jesus Christ by Win Tuck-Gleason

Joy Of The Cross by Win Tuck-Gleason

Printed in the United States
by Baker & Taylor Publisher Services